Stockholm combines natural, rugged beauty with a vibrant city life. There are no clear boundaries between its lakes, forests, and parks, as well as its buildings, monuments, and subway stations. Creativity is found in every corner: just step inside the countless museums, restaurants, cafés, shops, and nightclubs to see it for yourself. A front-runner in fashion, music, and design, keep an eye on Stockholm, as it continually influences and moulds the artistic and cultural zeitgeist.

CITIx60: Stockholm explores the stunning Swedish capital in five aspects; covering architecture, art spaces, shops, markets, dining, and entertainment options. With expert advice from 60 stars of the local creative scene, this book guides you to the city's real attractions for an authentic taste of Stockholm life.

Contents

T0349806

Before You Go

BASIC INFO

Currency
Swedish Krona (SEK/kr)
Exchange rate: US$1 : ~9.5 SEK

Time zone
GMT +1
DST +2*

*DST begins at 0200 (local time) on the last Sunday of March and ends at 0300 (local time) on the last Sunday of October.

Dialling
International calling: +46
Citywide: (0)8*

*Add (0) for calls made within Sweden.

Weather (avg. temperature range)
Spring (Mar–May): –3–16°C / 27–61°F
Summer (June–Aug): 10–21°C / 50–70°F
Autumn (Sep–Nov): 1–14°C / 34–57°F
Winter (Dec–Feb): –4–1°C / 25–34°F

USEFUL WEBSITES

Public transport info & travel planner
sl.se

Tax free shopping guide & refund calculator
www.globalblue.com/destinations/sweden

Festivals & shows ticketing
www.ticnet.se

EMERGENCY CALLS

Ambulance, fire or police
112

Embassies
France   +46 (0)8 459 53 00
Germany   +46 (0)8 670 15 00
Japan   +46 (0)8 579 353 00
Spain   +46 (0)8 522 808 00
UK   +46 (0)8 671 30 00
US   +46 (0)8 783 53 00

AIRPORT EXPRESS TRANSFERS

Arlanda Airport <–> Stockholm Central Station (Arlanda Express)
Trains / Journey: Every 10–15 mins / 20 mins
From Arlanda Airport – 0450–0105*
From Stockholm Central Station (Platforms 1 & 2) – 0420–0035*
One-way: 295 SEK / Return: 570 SEK
www.arlandaexpress.com

Skavsta Airport <–> Stockholm City Terminal (Flygbussarna Airport Coaches)
Buses / Journey: Every 20–60 mins / 80 mins
From Skavsta Airport – 0740–2355*
From Stockholm City Terminal – 0330–1830*
One-way: 179 SEK / Return: 325 SEK*
www.flygbussarna.se

*Departure times may vary on specific days. Fare discounts available on website. Please check for updates online before your journey.

PUBLIC TRANSPORT IN STOCKHOLM

Subway/metro
Light rail
Commuter train
Bus
Tram
Ferry

Means of Payment
Credit card
Cash

PUBLIC HOLIDAYS

January	1 New Year's Day, 6 Epiphany
Mar/Apr	Good Friday, Easter Monday
May	1 May Day, Ascension Day
June	6 National Day, Pentecost, Midsummer's Eve & Day
Oct/Nov	All Saints' Day
December	24 Christmas Eve, 25 Christmas Day, 26 Boxing Day, 31 New Year's Eve

*Museums and galleries are likely to take summer breaks between June and August.

FESTIVALS / EVENTS

February
Stockholm Design Week
www.stockholmdesignweek.com

April
Stockholm Art Week
stockholmartweek.se
Kulturnatt Stockholm
kulturnattstockholm.se

June
Summerburst Festival
summerburst.se/stockholm

July
Stockholm Pride
www.stockholmpride.org
Stockholm Street Festival
stockholmstreetfestival.com

August
Popaganda
www.popaganda.se
Midnattsloppet
www.midnattsloppet.com
Stockholm Music & Arts Festival
stockholmmusicandarts.com
Stockholms Kulturfestival
kulturfestivalen.stockholm.se

September
Stockholm Beer & Whiskey Festival
www.stockholmbeer.se

October
Stockholm Jazz Festival
www.stockholmbeer.se

November
Stockholm International Film Festival
www.stockholmfilmfestival.se

December
Nobel Week
www.nobelprize.org

*Event days vary by year. Please check for updates online.

UNUSUAL OUTINGS

The Green Trails
thegreentrails.com

Stockholm Ghost Walk
www.stockholmghostwalk.com

Rooftop Tours
www.takvandring.com

Historical Tram Tours
www.djurgardslinjen.se

Stieg Larsson Millennium Tour
stadsmuseet.stockholm.se/in-english/guided-tours/the-millennium-tour--the-girl-with-the-dragon-tattoo/

ABBA City Walk
stadsmuseet.stockholm.se/in-english/guided-tours/abba-city-walk

SMARTPHONE APPS

Public transport tickets
SL-Reseplanerare och Biljetter

Archipelago ferry ticket info & timetables
Waxholmsbolaget

WiFi hotspot locator
WiFi Spots

Journey planner
STHLM Traveling (Android), Res i STHLM

REGULAR EXPENSES

A double espresso
20-30 SEK

A traditional Swedish breakfast
65-100 SEK

Gratuities
At restaurants & bars (with no service charge):
Round up to the nearest 10 SEK
For licensed taxis: 5-10% of payment

Count to 10

What makes Stockholm so special?

Illustrations by Guillaume Kashima aka Funny Fun

Stockholm is well-known for being at the forefront of style: think mini-malist fashion, cutting-edge music, and sustainable design. Amid all things contemporary and cool, nature still makes its presence strongly felt in the city - where youngsters take midnight dips in Lake Mälaren, just a few steps away from the Central Station. Whether you are on a one-day stopover or a week-long stay, see what Stockholm creatives consider essential to see, taste, and take home from your trip.

1

Architecture

Hötorgsskraporna (Building 5)
by Backström & Reinius

Skogskyrkogården (#9)
*by Gunnar Asplund &
Sigurd Lewerentz*

Artipelag (#15)
by Nyréns Arkitektkontor

**Årstabroarna
(Western Årsta Bridge)**
by Norman Foster

Stockholms Stadsbibliotek (#5)
by Gunnar Asplund

Ferry Terminal @ Strömkajen
by Marge Arkitekter

2
New Art Encounters

Konsthall C
Feminist, queer & political art
www.konsthallc.se

FFAR
Architectural gallery & forums
www.ffar.se

Gallery Steinsland Berliner
Contemporary art
www.steinslandberliner.com

Grafikens Hus
Graphic art prints
www.grafikenshus.se

Editions in Craft
New take on traditional crafts
www.editionsincraft.com

Fylkingen
New music & intermedia art
wwww.fylkingen.se

3
The Archipelago
stockholmarchipelago.se

Vaxholm
Vikings, herrings & fortifications

Nynäshamn
Local delicacies & one of Sweden's best
surfing beaches

Ängsö
Sweden's first & smallest national park,
rich flora & fauna

Dalarö
Water adventures (esp. diving, sailing,
kayaking), gingerbread architecture

Landsort
Seal & eagle safari, sculpture park,
Plague Cemetery

Vifärnaholme
Free space for creative projects
ideasisland.com

Grinda
Rocky cliffs, woody forests, picnic spots

4
A Day in Djurgården

Rosenlunds Trädgård
Beautiful café & eco garden
www.rosendalstradgard.se

Gröna Lund
Amusement park
www.gronalund.com

Skansen
First open-air museum & zoo
www.skansen.se

MDT
Contemporary choreography
mdtsthlm.se

Thielska Galleriet
Beautiful museum in a wealthy
art patron's former residence
www.thielska-galleriet.se

Moderna Museet (#16)

5

Classic Food

Tunnbrödsrulle (Swedish-style hot dog with shrimp salad)
Any snack bar or stand

Herring & snaps
Sturehof
www.sturehof.com

Meatballs
Tranan, www.tranan.se
Pelikan (#40)

Kräftor (crayfish)
Urban Deli
www.urbandeli.org

Fried Baltic herring
Strömmingsvagnen
Kornhamnstorg, 111 27

Kanelbullar (cinnamon rolls)
Tössebageriet, tosse.se
Rosendals Tradgard
www.rosendalstradgard.se/kafe

6

Fika Spots

Drop Coffee
Coffee roastery & coffee bar
www.dropcoffee.com

Spånga Konditori
Coffee & cakes
www.spangakonditori.se

Konditori Ritorno
Pastries & ambience
www.ritorno.se

Chutney
Vegetarian food & vegan pastries
chutney.se

Johan & Nyströms
Weekly coffee choices
johanochnystrom.se

Kafé 44
vegan food, coffee & show nights
kafe44.org

7

Locally Made Products

Dalahäst (wooden horse)
Wooden Horse Museum
woodenhorsemuseumsweden.se

Bikes & accessories
BIKEID
bikeid.se

Toffees & caramel candies
Pärlans Konfektyr
www.parlanskonfektyr.se

Handmade glass & ceramics
blås & knåda
www.blasknada.com

Perfume, body care & fragrances
Byredo Parfume
byredo.com

Specialty craft beers
Omnipollos Hatt (#58)

Mohawk beer
mohawkbrewing.se

8

Seasonal Activities

Celebrate Midsommar
sweden.se/culture-traditions/
midsummer

**Summerbio (summer cinema)
@Rålambshovsparken**
www.stockholmfilmfestival.se

Picnic on the rocks of Fredhäll
Bring a disposable BBQ grill &
throw on a couple of *korv med
bröd* (sausages with bread)

**Eat semlor (traditional almond
paste-filled buns) on Shrove
Tuesday**
Linquists Konditori
www.lindquists.nu

**Go for an ice plunge or
sauna in the winter**
Hellasgården
www.hellasgarden.se

Skate on frozen lakes
The Stockholm archipelago (#12)

9

Leisurely Routes

View graffiti on the Pendeltåg
Between the Spånga & Karlberg
stations, sl.se

**View Gamla Stan (#6) &
the City Hall (#7)**
From the Monteliusvägen
walkway

Explore the city by bicycle
Along Årstabroarna (the Årsta
bridges), Västerbron (the
Western bridge), Norr & Söder
Mälarstrand (Northern Shore of
Mälaren); around Årstaviken; or in
Skeppsholmen

**Go on a dinner cruise to
Vaxholm**
www.blidosundsbolaget.se/en/
dinner-cruises/

**Stroll along a waterfront
boulevard**
Strandvägen, Östermalm

10

Homegrown Labels

Backpacks, tote bags, wallets
Sandqvist
www.sandqvist.net

Fashionable ready-to-wear
Acne Studios (#30)
Filippa K, www.filippa-k.com

Sneakers
Eytys
www.eytys.com

Sustainable looks for men
Uniforms for the Dedicated
uniformsforthededicated.com

Clean fashion & denim designs
Weekday
www.weekday.com

Fun women's basics
Monki
www.monki.com

Icon Index

 Opening hours

 Admission

Address

 Facebook

Contact

 Instagram

Remarks

 Website

 Scan QR codes to access Google Maps and discover the area around each destination. Internet connection required.

60x60

60 Local Creatives x 60 Hotspots

From its vast and colourful cityscapes to the tiniest glimpses of everyday exchanges, there is much inspiration to be found in and around Stockholm. 60x60 points you to 60 haunts where 60 local arbiters of taste find theirs.

Landmarks & Architecture — SPOTS · 01 – 12 📍

Nature is in the heart of Stockholm's city life. Take a ferry and discover the rustic Swedish archipelago. Explore Modernist and Nordic Classical buildings from the likes of Gunnar Asplund.

Cultural & Art Spaces — SPOTS · 13 – 24 📍

Take in modern art and photography, then relish in classical Scandinavian paintings at the city's vibrant museums and galleries. Stockholm is at the forefront of music, design, and art.

Markets & Shops — SPOTS · 25 – 36 📍

Stockholm is a treasure trove of vintage ephemera, minimalist fashion, and design shops. Take your pick from retro accessories, stunning textiles, or quirky books bound by hand.

Restaurants & Cafés — SPOTS · 37 – 48 📍

Coffee and cake lovers will have their hands full in the city. Indulge in lavish Swedish cuisine, or tuck into some hearty street eats. Don't leave without eating a **kannelbulle.**

Nightlife — SPOTS · 49 – 60 📍

Catch a live gig at an intimate venue, enjoy crafted cocktails with stunning views of the sunset, or go for a midnight dip. A fantastic night out awaits, no matter what your fun may be.

Landmarks & Architecture

Nordic Classicism, a charming Old Town, and idyllic islands

Straddling Lake Mälaren and the Baltic Sea, Stockholm's unique landscape is a sight to behold. Wide avenues and tall 19th-century buildings, combined with shimmering bodies of water and sporadic forests, exude vastness and tranquility. One is never truly far from nature in the city, as seen in the works of Swedish architects such as Gunnar Asplund's (1885-1940) creations. Surrounded by trees and sloping fields, his stunning woodland cemetery Skogskyrkogården (#9), brings together modern architecture in the Nordic Classicist style and equally beautiful natural surroundings. It is a perfect place for an introspective morning walk and quiet reflection. In the afternoon, explore the cobblestone streets of Gamla Stan (#6) for a glimpse of its famed medieval architecture and a taste of local history before pausing for *fika* at one of the many cosy cellar cafés in the vicinity. During the warmer months, pack a picnic basket and take a stroll up the rocky cliffs of Skinnarviksberget (#11), Stockholm's highest natural point, for a spectacular view of the skyline. Beyond the city, a trip to Stockholm would not be complete without an excursion to the picturesque islands of the Stockholm Archipelago (#12). Ideas Island in Vifärnaholme offers an idyllic base for creatives to work and stay inspired; while Värmdö houses the Artipelag (#15) – a must for both architecture and nature lovers. The scenic boat trip to the islands will already be an experience in itself.

Filmhuset
P.016

Martin Falck
Graphic designer

I am a graphic designer and visual researcher working with print design, music, art direction, video, fashion, and animation.

Ramiro Oblitas
Cofounder, Parasol

I am a quadrilingual graphic design and branding specialist with 15+ years of international experience working across sectors including aviation, public transport, and retail.

Anders Kornestedt
Partner, Happy F&B

Happy F&B's mission is to nurture and release great ideas. By marrying a far-sighted strategy with design, we help develop brands that make a world of real difference.

Stockholms Tunnelbana
P.014

Sven-Harrys Konst-museum
P.017

Daniel Mair
Creative consultant & designer

I run my own multidisciplinary studio Mair / Wennel and teach at Konstfack in Stockholm. After living in London for ten years, I see and appreciate Stockholm in a different way.

Stockholms Stads-bibliotek
P.019

Hannah Waldron
Artist & designer

To me, weaving is a natural process to complement my grid-based images. I am currently a research student in Craft at Konstfack, investigating how weaving tells stories.

FORM US WITH LOVE
Design studio

For the last decade, we have put dialogue and relevance at the core, using clever design to position, build, and sustain brands of tomorrow. Past collaborators include Ikea, Muuto, and Absolut.

Ericsson Globe
P.018

Gamla Stan
P.020

Clara von Zweigbergk
Art director & product designer

I was born in Stockholm and work as a graphic designer. I am currently in pursuit of my great interest in paper, colour, typography, and form.

Markuskyrkan
P.024

David Ericsson
DAVID ERICSSON Design Studio

For me, "zeitgeist" is important because we are living in a time of change. Besides DAVID ERICSSON, I also co-founded DMOCH and teach at Carl Malmsten Furniture Studies.

Jonas Wagell
Architect & designer

My studio is in Hornstull, but recent projects reach as far as Asia and North America. Our work with products and architecture has been recognised as simplistic playfulness and clever compact living.

Stadshuset
P.021

Skogskyrkogården
P.025

Herr Nilsson
Street artist

I am a visual activist based in Stockholm. I am most known for my Dark Princess series, violent Winnie the Pooh, and Hello Kitty paintings.

Skinnarviksberget
P.028

Anna Lidberg
Founder, Gallery 1:10

Besides curation, I create video installations, objects, and social projects,; often exploring issues of art's accessibility, power structures, and their relationship with the spectator.

Oskar Lübeck
Founder, Bold

I am the founder and executive creative director of design agency Bold. After some years abroad, I now spend most of my time on Södermalm, where I live with my wife and two kids.

Tranebergsbron
P.026

Stockholms
Skärgård
P.029

1 Stockholms Tunnelbana

Engulfed in mosaics, paintings, installations, and engravings, Stockholm's subway stations have been a spectacle since the 1950s. The first stations were built during a time of socialist influence over politics as well as the dream and belief in the welfare state. More than 150 artists have left their voices in over 90 stations since then – turning public art into historical monuments. If you do not have the time to station-hop, be sure to at least stop by the Kungsträdgården where rescued relics tell stories of Stockholm's past, and Östermalmstorg where Siri Derkert saluted women's rights, world peace, and the green movement.

🕐 *Opening hours vary by station* 🔗 *sl.se*
🔗 *Free 1-hr guided tour: 1500 (Tu, Th, Sa) [Jun-Aug]. Info: sl.se/en/eng-info/contact/art-walks*

"The trip from the inner city to the outer suburbs is amazing. There is a guided tour but my advice would be to just travel by yourself and really go everywhere."
– Martin Falck

2 Filmhuset
Map H, P.109

Conceived by Peter Celsing (1920–1974), the Swedish Film Institute building completed in 1970 is typical for the architect's brutalist style. The abundance of concrete surfaces, filmstrip-inspired window frames, and film reel-like stairwells were all Celsing's riposte to the founder's request for 'no ordinary bloody building' to promote film-making and appreciation. Architecture buffs should also take a stroll in the Gärdet area to contemplate more great buildings from the era, like the Kaknäs Tower at Mörka Kroken 28-30, and Garnisonen, an expansive office complex at Karlavägen 100.

🕐 🅢 *Check website for film info*
🏠 *Borgvägen 1-5, 115 53*
📞 *+46 (0)8 665 1100*
🔗 *www.sfi.se/filmhuset*

"This is one of Peter Celsing's public buildings that present radical modernism with a lot of intellectual layers."

– Anders Kornestedt, Happy F&B

3 Sven-Harrys Konstmuseum
Map A, P.104

Instead of donating to another museum, art collector Sven-Harry Karlsson decided to build one of his very own next to Vasaparken. Designed by Wingårdhs Architects, its gleaming brass-clad facade beckons the public within – where Karlsson's personal collections are housed in a replica of his former home on the roof of the building. A sculpture-filled terrace that offers stunning city and park views is also open to visitors when the weather permits. In the lower galleries, multifaceted exhibitions of Swedish contemporary artists rotate yearly.

🕐 1100–1900 (W, F), –2100 (Th), –1700 (Sa–Su)
💲 170 SEK incl. Karlsson's home/120/Free for 18-
🏠 Eastmansvägen 10–12, 113 61
📞 +46 (0)8 511 600 60　🔗 www.sven-harrys.se
📘 @svenharryskonstmuseum　🖋 Karlsson's home is open for tours only. Check website for info.

"The exterior is cladded in a metal called Nordic Royal.
The yellow facade is truly fantastic."

– Ramiro Oblitas, Parasol

4 Ericsson Globe
Map C, P.105

The Sweden Solar System was brought into being by Nils Brenning and Gösta Gahm, who deemed the Ericsson Globe – the largest hemispherical building in the world – the Sun. As the largest permanent scale model of its kind, the System spans the entire country and continues to grow as artists interpret the different planets, accurately resized and spaced out to the scale of 1:20 million. Nearby, the Stockholm City Museum hosts Mercury, a 25cm-in-diameter metallic sphere that is heated to symbolise its proximity to the Sun. Opened in 1989, the Ericsson Globe is also a live performance and sports arena that can accommodate over 15,000 fans.

🏠 Globentorget, 121 77
URL swedensolarsystem.se
🔗 Events: www.stockholmlive.com

"Visit the Sweden Solar System site and use it as a guide. The Globe looks best from Södermalm – no point in going up close."
– Daniel Mair

5 Stockholms Stadsbibliotek
Map A, P.104

Designed by Gunnar Asplund (1885-1940) and opened in 1928, the Stockholm City Library was the first in the country to offer public access to its bookstacks. The building itself features a rotunda sitting atop a plinth-like cube; creating a simple yet striking geometric structure that has been considered to be a stark Nordic Classicist composition. With its endless tiers of books, tailor-made furniture, open spaces, and cosy sections, locals from all walks of life flock within its walls for a day well spent. To appreciate the full extent of the architect's ambitions and work, take a stroll in the surrounding park.

🕙 1000-1900 (M-F), 1200-1600 (Sa)
📍 Sveavägen 73, 113 80 📞 +46 (0)8 508 309 00
🔗 biblioteket.stockholm.se 👤 @stadsbiblioteket

"Beautiful circular building designed by Gunnar Asplund."
– Hannah Waldron

6 Gamla Stan
Map D, P.106

Skip the touristy Västerlånggatan and wander
through the narrow streets of Gamla Stan,
where Stockholm was found in 1252. Medieval
alleyways, cobblestone streets, and archaic
architecture give this area its unique identity
as the city's Old Town, where charming little
shops, eateries, and bars offer you the chance
to catch an eccentric live jazz performance,
or settle into a Chesterfield armchair for a
comfy night out. Make time for landmarks like
the Stockholm Cathedral, Nobel Museum, and
Riddarholmen Church – a former monastery
on the adjacent island of Riddarholmen – then
round up your trip with some authentic Nordic
home cooking at Den Gyldene Freden.

URL *Den Gyldene Freden: gyldenefreden.se,
Stampen: www.stampen.se,
Tweed: www.tweedbar.se*

*"Eat at Den Gyldene Freden to fully experience
the old vibe."*

– FORM US WITH LOVE

7 Stadshuset

Map F, P.108

An iconic National Romantic masterpiece, the Stockholm City Hall adds a touch of royalty to the skyline by holding the Swedish royals' Three Crowns 106 metres up in the air above its lantern-topped spire. Designed by Ragnar Östberg, guided tours offer the only chance for the public to view its ceremonial halls, most notably, the Golden Hall with its 18 million gold mosaic tiles and the Blue Hall, where the annual Nobel Prize banquet takes place. The City Hall Tower and Tower Museum are worth the climb.

🕐 City Hall Tours: 1000–1500 (hourly) (Tower & Tower Museum: 0910–1550/1710 (40-min intervals)) 💲 120/100/40 SEK (Apr-Oct), 90/80/40 SEK (Nov-Mar) (Tower: 60 SEK) 🏠 Hantverkargatan 1, 111 52 📞 +46 (0)8 508 290 58 🌐 international. stockholm.se/the-city-hall 🖇 No booking required for tours. Check website for info.

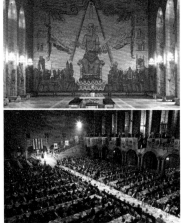

"The garden stairs lead right into the water – perfect for a swim!"

– Clara von Zweigbergk

8 Markuskyrkan
Map M, P.110

Set amid a birch grove away from the non-descript apartments that characterise Björkhagen, Markuskyrkan embodies architect Sigurd Lewerentz's (1885–1975) aspirations to establish symbolism through materiality, craftsmanship, and the use of light. Within the beautiful 1960s brickwork building, this becomes clear as one wanders from daylight into darkness through its multiple recesses. Architectural details, decorative works, as well as bespoke fittings and finishings magically reveal themselves as the eyes slowly adapt to the pitch-black nave.

🕓 *Under renovation until Sept 2019. Check website for updated info.* 🏠 *Malmövägen 51, 121 53* 🕓 *+46 (0)8 505 815 00* 🔳 *www.svenskakyrkan.se/skarpnack/markuskyrkan*

"After visiting the church, you can walk about 25 minutes and see the UNESCO World Heritage site, Skogskyrkogården (#9)."

– David Ericsson, DAVID ERICSSON Design Studio

9 Skogskyrkogården
Map O, P.110

Stretching out across a vast park area, the Woodland Cemetery was realised as a new memorial garden concept in the early 1900s by main architects Gunnar Asplund and Sigurd Lewerentz. Natural beauty and artistic sensibilities complement one another to create harmony and tranquility in this multi-ethnic UNESCO World Heritage burial ground. While the chapels and crematoriums can only be visited via guided tours, the cemetery itself is always open for long strolls of contemplation. To get here, take the bus that leaves every hour from outside the Skogskyrkogården subway station.

🏠 *Sockenvägen, 122 33* 🔗 *skogskyrkogarden. stockholm.se* 📞 *+46 (0)8 508 317 30* ✐ *Guided tours: 1030 (Su) (Jul–Sep) @ 150 SEK. Advanced booking recommended. Check website for info.*

"*Some of Sweden's leading architects and artists were involved in the creation and artistic decoration of the cemetery.*"

– Jonas Wagell

10 Tranebergsbron

Map L, P.110

Spanning a length of 450 metres, the 1934 Traneberg Bridge built by modernist architect Paul Hedqvist (1895–1977) once boasted the world's largest concrete vault. A road and pedestrian sidewalk are situated on the bridge for crossing the Tranebergssund strait; commanding a stunning panorama of the central part of Stockholm. The underside of the bridge is also worth checking out for its gigantic pillars, where street art is repeatedly created and quickly cleaned. Take the subway to Alvik station and follow Tranebergsvägen to a dirt road that leads to the foundation of the bridge. Painters be warned: the bridge is constantly under the Commuter Security guard's watch.

🏠 *Alvik, Kristineberg*

"*The urban sounds of traffic 30 metres above, the beautiful view of the city, and the waterfront make this my favourite place in Stockholm.*"

– Herr Nilsson

11 Skinnarviksberget

Map I, P.109

At over 50 metres, Skinnarviksberget is Stockholm's highest natural point, where you can escape the urban grind and take in beautiful panoramas of central Stockholm. It is popular for barbecues, picnics, sunset views, and parties at dusk – particularly during the warmer months of the year. Nearby, the Ivar Los Park at Bastugatan 26 also offers stunning sights of the city, with traces of the Söder area's working class history. Take Tavastgatan and drop by Teenage Engineering's showroom at no. 15.

🏠 *Söder Mälarstrand, 118 23*

"If you wish to bring your own alcoholic drinks, the best place to get them is Systembolaget. It closes in the evening and most of the weekends, so plan ahead."

– Anna Lidberg, Gallery 1:10

12 Stockholms Skärgård

A tourist destination in its own right, no trip to Stockholm is complete without exploring the rugged natural beauty of its archipelago. With 30,000 small islands of picturesque, largely untouched woods, rocky cliffs, and sandy beaches, it is a unique and truly inspiring place that will bring out your inner explorer. Outdoor pursuits like fishing, hiking, cycling, camping, and swimming are popular, as are arts and cultural encounters. Tailor your own unforgettable trip or go to Count to 10 on p.005 for highlights.

URL stockholmarchipelago.se

"Torö is my all-time favourite. My wife and I fell so hard or the island that we bought a vacation house there. It's known for its waves, and Stenstrand has the best."

– Oskar Lübeck, Bold

Cultural & Art Spaces

Trendsetting art, splendid photography, and melancholic classics

A city where creativity is seen and felt almost everywhere, Stockholm takes the lead in the international arts and design scene, with its residents being setters and early adopters of global trends. Sustainability, innovation, and openness are values that resonate with Swedish thinking, ideas, and creative pursuits. Bask in the beauty of modern photography at Fotografiska (#17) or keep up with the latest in contemporary art, fashion, and design at Liljevalchs (#21). If it is natural beauty that captures your imagination, take a boat trip to Artipelag (#15), located in the Swedish archipelago. Its modern architecture combined with the rugged beauty of the surrounding lake and forest, is breathtaking. Modern art lovers should also visit Moderna Museet (#16) and the neighbouring ArkDes for a slice of architectural history. In addition to the two, Djurgården island is filled to the brim with excellent (and more classical) museums including Vasamuseet, Prins Eugens Waldemarsudde, and Thielska Galleriet. The moody late-19th and early-20th century painting collections at the latter two capture the essence of the Swedish soul. To round up your art-filled day, check out the performance listings at Färgfabriken (#14), housed in a former colour-making factory, for experimental art exhibitions, concerts, and regular flea markets.

Jenny Theolin
Owner, Studio Theolin

I am an active writer, creative director, curator, and producer heading up StudioTheolin that specialises in visual arts, music, and culture. I also run an MA programme at Hyper Island.

Färgfabriken
P.035

Fredrik Wikholm
Uniforms for the Dedicated

I co-founded and creatively direct both the label and initiative, The Ragbag. Sustainability, music, people, and challenges are dear to me. Stockholm is great but even greater coming back to.

Johanna Irander
Founder, Studio Irander

I set up Studio Irander in The Hague in 2007. The office is currently based in Stockholm, working within the fields of landscape architecture and urban planning.

Kulturhuset
Stads-
teatern
P.034

Artipelag
P.036

Stockholm Design Lab
Branding agency

SDL transforms brands and businesses with simple, remarkable ideas. We keep an unswerving focus on what lasts – on truth, not triviality, and on intelligence, not speculation.

Fotografiska
P.039

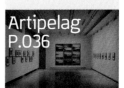

Fredric Benesch & Katarina Lundeberg

We are architects, critics, and the founders of In Praise of Shadows Arkitektur, engaged in several housing projects and Aesop stores. We also teach at the KTH Architecture School.

Sara N Bergman
Illustrator

I am a children's book illustrator, and stylist and designer of Love Warriors. I was born in southern Sweden and moved here in the 1990s. I love every part of my job and my hometown.

Moderna
Museet
P.038

Magasin III
P.040

Emma Löfström
Artist

I am an image-maker, working with drawings and collage whilst exploring multilayered human conditions. I have partaken in The White Building's Iaspis residency programme in 2015.

Carl Eldh Studio Museum
P.042

Rui Tenreiro
Author, illustrator & art director

I create narrative experiences through storytelling, be it through a book, film, or piece of writing.

Marabou-parken
P.041

Jens Assur
Photographer & filmmaker

I work as a still photographer and filmmaker driven by an inexhaustible curiosity about our contemporary world. Through my work, I spur people on to reflect about how we live our lives.

Liljevalchs
P.043

Lisa Ullenius & Sissi Edholm, *Edholm Ullenius*

We are a graphic design and illustration studio that sees the result of every project as a pure dialogue with lust and surprise. Since 2002, our clients range from Ikea and Paul Smith.

Kultur-föreningen Tellus
P.046

Marcus Lindeen
Writer & director

I write and direct films and theatre plays. My work is mostly based on documentary materials, so I spend a lot of time on research and interviews. I am about to move to Midsommarkransen.

Veronica Wallenberg
Director, Cinematic

I am a director at animation studio Cinematic. I am also a huge travel enthusiast and will spend big parts of the year travelling albeit mostly working at the same time.

Hallwylska Museet
P.044

Seriegalleriet
P.047

13 Kulturhuset Stadsteatern
Map F, P.108

Architect Peter Celsing's vision to create an accessible 'culture lounge' was finally realised when Kulturhuset opened in 1974. Often compared to the Centre Pompidou in Paris, the complex building encourages visitors to navigate the space over several floors. Alongside an ambitious programme of modern theatre, art exhibitions, and literary events, Kulturhuset also runs interesting activities on a smaller scale. Parkteatern is one such highlight; welcoming visitors of all ages to enjoy performance theatre in a less formal, outdoor setting.

🕐 Info Centre: 1100–1800 (M–F), –1600 (Sa–Su)
🏠 Info Centre: Under Fontänen, Sergels Torg, 103 27
📞 +46 (0)8 506 202 00 URL kulturhusetstadsteatern.se
f @kulturhusetstadsteatern ⊘ Main site is under renovation but programmes are on-going. Check with Info Centre or online for info & locations.

"Take time to visit its wonderful roof-top terrace. It's perfect for an arty meander, a read in the library, or a G&T in the sun."

– Jenny Theolin, Studio Theolin

14 Färgfabriken
Map G, P.108

Situated close to the water in Liljeholmen and housed in a former colour-making factory, Färgfabriken shows you a different side of town. A charming and slightly off-the-grid art gallery just a 10 minute-walk from Liljeholmen Station, the venue hosts everything from experimental art exhibitions to flea markets. If possible, check out their club nights or parties, which are gathering points for creative Stockholmers. Stop by the Färgfabrikens Kafé for drinks and a spot of people-watching.

🕐 💲 *Gallery: 1100–1900 (Th), –1600 (F), –1700 (Sa–Su) during exhibitions only. Check online for updated info.* 🏠 *Lövholmsbrinken 1, 117 43* 📞 *+46 (0)8 645 0707* 🔗 *fargfabriken.se* 🇫 *@fargfabriken* 📎 *The café usually closes in the summer.*

"Come for experimental exhibitions in art and architecture."
– Johanna Irander, Studio Irander

15 Artipelag
Map K, P.110

Whether by boat in the summer, or by car in the winter, the journey to Artipelag is breath-taking. Designed by the late architect Johan Nyrén and opened in 2012, the 3,000 square-metre space has much to offer for those who are interested in art as much as nature and architecture. Classical and contemporary expressions merge into rotating exhibitions and programmed activities that engage with their idyllic surroundings. Soak in the vibes as you head up to the rooftop and enjoy a weekend brunch with scenic views over Baggen's Bay.

🕐 1100-1700 (M-W, Sa-Su), -1900 (Th-F)
💲 235/180 SEK combo price for all exhibitions. Free for 15- 🏠 Artipelagstigen 1, 134 40 ☎ +46 (0)8 570 130 00 🔗 artipelag.se ❤ @artipelag
✎ Opening hours vary by season.

"It is an amazing, inspiring space for art and culture right out in the archipelago. Peace-giving in all the right ways."

– Fredrik Wikholm, Uniforms for the Dedicated & The Ragbag

16 Moderna Museet

Map D, P.106

Ideally situated on Skeppsholmen island, the Museum of Modern Art houses Swedish and international contemporary art as well as one of the largest specialised libraries for Nordic art, photography, and design. Gaze at Swedish painter Nils Dardel's post-impressionist gem 'The Dying Dandy' (1918) and marvel at its intensity of colours and emotions, alongside key pieces by Duchamp, Magritte, as well as a model of the Tatlin's Tower. Complete your trip by dropping by ArkDes, the Swedish Centre for Architecture and Design, next door.

🕙 1000–2000 (Tu, F), –1800 (W–Th, Sa–Su)
💲 Prices vary by exhibition 🏠 Exercisplan 4, 111 49
📞 +46 (0)8 520 235 00 🔗 modernamuseet.se
📘 @ModernaMuseet 🎧 Download the Audio Guide app for free. Opening hours vary by season.

"The museum was first opened in 1958 and, in 2004, Stockholm Design Lab designed its current visual identity."

– Stockholm Design Lab

17 Fotografiska
Map E, P.107

Presenting four major exhibitions annually, alongside a number of minor exhibitions, Fotografiska is the only institution in Stockholm that focuses purely on photography. Past events include a retrospective of American portrait photographer Annie Leibovitz, and a curated exhibition of polaroid portraits by acclaimed filmmaker Gus Van Sant. The museum also boasts a renowned restaurant which is an experience in itself, where flavours, scents, materials, and ambience are all part of a carefully prepared package. Diners can bask in the spectacular view over the lake and enjoy occasional live music in the summer.

🕐 0900–2300 (Su–W), –0100 (Th–Sa) [Restaurant: 1700–2300 (Tu–Sa)]
💲 165 SEK/Free for 12–
🏠 Stadsgårdshamnen 22, 116 45
☎ +46 (0)8 509 005 00
🔗 www.fotografiska.com
📘 @fotografiskasto
🔗 Card payments only. Advance ticket purchase via website recommended.

"Shop in the day and visit the museum at night since it opens till late. The view from the restaurant is stunning. Book ahead if you want a table indoors!"

– Sara N Bergman

18 Magasin III

Lodged into an old warehouse on a former freeport, Magasin III was home to Stockholm's most edgy modern art collections, featuring everything from art by Ai WeiWei to dreamy video installations by Pipilotti Rist. Besides functioning as a contemporary art foundation, the museum also offered a masters degree programme in art curation with Stockholm University. Although it still operates a satellite space in Tel Aviv, its public programme is currently under review as the founders look for new ways to engage with visitors in the near future. In the meantime, its on-going newsletter is well worth the subscription for its fresh takes on the global arts scene.

🕙 💲 *Check online for updated info*
📞 +46 (0)8 545 680 40
🔗 *www.magasin3.com* 📘 *@magasin3*

"Look into their drawing collection and fantastic library of art books."

– Fredric Benesch & Katarina Lundeberg, In Praise of Shadows Arkitektur

19 Marabouparken
Map J, P.110

What used to be Marabou's cocoa laboratory and chocolate factory is now a lively meeting place for contemporary art. Built in the 1950s, the Marabouparken art gallery regularly engages artists and visitors to explore and reflect on issues in today's society through themed workshops, forums, and film programmes, alongside artist collaborations scattered throughout the Arthur von Schmalensee-designed space. Check online for kid-friendly events in the gallery and surrounding park.

🕐 1200–2000 (W), –1700 (Th-Su)
[Park: 0800–2100 (May-Oct), 0900–1700 (Nov-Apr)] 💲 70 SEK
🏠 Löfströmsvägen 8, 172 66
📞 +46 (0)8 294 590
🌐 marabouparken.se
f @Marabouparken

"Attached to the gallery is a beautiful sculpture park initially installed as a recreational facility for the factory workers in the 1950s."

– Emma Löfström

041

20 Carl Eldh Studio Museum
Map A, P.104

Designed in 1919 by the same architect responsible for the Stadhuset or Stockholm City Hall (#7), Carl Eldh Ateljémuseum honours one of Sweden's pre-eminent sculptors in the early 20th century. This unconventional wooden building used to be the artist's home and studio space, which currently preserves busts, sketches, and original models of his most renowned masterpieces like The Titan and The Branting Monument. Besides learning more about his life (1873-1954) and work, visitors can also take in the beauty of its hilltop site at the café or in the sculpture-filled garden.

🕐 1200-1600 (Tu-Th) excl. 21-22 June
🅢 100 SEK/Free for 15- 🏠 Lögebodavägen 10, 113 47
📞 +46 (0)8 612 6560 URL www.eldhsatelje.se
f @carleldhsateljemuseum1919

"This museum is relatively unknown and deserves a supporting visit for the beauty and space."
– Rui Tenreiro

21 Liljevalchs
Map B, P.105

Girdled by the beautiful natural surroundings of Djurgården, the Liljevalchs art gallery was established in 1916 as the first independent, public museum for contemporary art in Sweden. Designed by Carl Bergsten, its presents at least four large exhibitions each year showcasing contemporary art, fashion, and design trends, alongside the famous juried Vårsalongen (Spring Salon) event. Be sure to browse around the museum store for quirky design souvenirs. Nearby, Prins Eugens Waldemarsudde and Thielska Galleriet are also worth taking a peek into for classical Swedish paintings.

🕐 1000-1700 (M-F), 1100- (Sa-Su) 💲 80 SEK/Free for 18- 🏠 Djurgårdsvägen 60, 115 21 ☎ +46 (0)8 508 313 30 URL www.liljevalchs.se f @liljevalchs
🖉 Opening hours vary by season.

"Visit Liljevalchs during its famous Spring Salon, where non-professionals come to show their work to a grand audience. Everything is for sale, at reasonable prices."

– Jens Assur

22 Hallwylska Museet
Map D, P.106

Escape to a different time as you visit the grand former home of Count Walther and Countess Wilhelmina von Hallwyl. One of the most expensive private residences ever built in Sweden, the home was completed in 1898 and later turned into a museum. Hallwlyska Museet houses the family's personal art, porcelain, and jewellery collections dating from the early 20th century. Take a peek inside its preserved rooms from the late-Victorian period in Sweden for a glimpse into the lavish lifestyles of the nobility in Stockholm at the time.

🕐 *1200–1600 (Tu, Th, F), –1900 (W), 1100–1700 (Sa–Su)*
🅂 *Fees may apply for tours & exhibitions*
🏠 *Hamngatan 4, 111 47* 📞 *+46 (0)8 402 3099*
🔗 *hallwylskamuseet.se* 📘 *@Hallwylskamuseet*
🖉 *Opening hours vary by season.*

"Step 100 years back in time!"

– Lisa Ullenius & Sissi Edholm, Edholm Ullenius

23 Kulturföreningen Tellus
Map N, P.110

Tellus is the true cultural heart of Midsommarkransen, an up-and-coming area in the south of Stockholm. The theatre opened at their current address in 1920 and was run as a commercial movie theatre until the mid-1980s, when it was taken over by a non-profit organisation. Tellus is one of the few independent cinemas left in Stockholm, but it offers much more than just film screenings. Events include after-work jazz concerts, poetry readings, art exhibitions, knitting clubs, game nights and language exchanges.

🕐 🅂 *Check online for programme info*
🏠 *Vattenledningsvägen 46, 126 33*
📞 *+46 (0)8 645 7551*
🔗 *www.tellusbio.nu*
f *@BiocafeTellus*

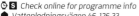

"Go to Midsommarkransen and walk around the neighbourhood. There is a little park called Svandammsparken and a great café for 'smørrebrød'."

– Marcus Lindeen

24 Seriegalleriet

Map I, P.109

Seriegalleriet sells original artwork from well-known comic books, picture books, and animated films. A haven for pop-culture enthusiasts and illustration aficionados, its mini exhibitions attract visitors in search of highly collectable, limited edition artwork. The gallery is located in the hip Södermalm area, between the Slussen and Mariatorget subway stations. It is also in close proximity to the bar at Rival Hotel, owned by ABBA star Benny Andersson, which is a great place to have a coffee or snack break in between shopping.

🕙 1100–1800 (M–F), 1200–1600 (Sa), 1300– (Su)
🏠 Sankt Paulsgatan 14, 118 46 📞 +46 (0)8 702 2425
🔗 www.seriegalleriet.se f @seriegalleriet

"You can always visit Staffars Serier around the corner (Bellmansgatan 26A) if you cannot get enough of this genre. They have lots of new and old comics."

– Veronica Wallenberg, Cinematic

Markets & Shops

Design goodies, vintage treasures, and quirky comics

Stockholm offers a wide array of boutiques and independent stores, with a spotlight on contemporary design and forward-thinking yet understated fashion. Take a whole day aside to do some shopping and exploring. The luxurious department store NK (*Hamngatan 18–20, 111 47*), housed in an impressive Art Nouveau building, offers Swedish designer clothing as well as furniture and home accessories from Design House Stockholm (*designhouse-stockholm.com*). Nearby, Åhléns is a good place to stock up on affordable souvenirs, accessories, stationery, and textiles. For mini-malist fashion, check out Our Legacy (#26) for menswear, APLACE (*www.aplace.com*) for the latest Scandinavian brands, and Acne Archive (*Torsgatan 53, 113 37*) for bargain steals on past collections. Grab a coffee, place yourself on Götgatan shopping street, where Swedish brands Weekday, Monki, and Filippa K are also located, and watch stylish pedestrians walk by for a dose of inspiration. While Stockholm is known as a fashion and design-lover's shopping paradise, it is also a vintage heaven in terms of quality and quantity. Spend an afternoon visiting the city's best thrift stores for bargains and one-of-a-kind accessories. Hunt the endless racks of clothing at Humana Second Hand (#33) for on-trend pieces at rock-bottom prices, as well as the popular Stockholm Stadsmission (*stadsmis-sionen.se*) and Beyond Retro (*www.beyondretro.com*) stores. For the ultimate collection of 1940s jewellery and vintage accessories, pop into Antikt Gammalt & Nytt (#35). Love comics? Step into Pa-percut (#29), a popular spot for collectors and illustration fans.

Lukas Rose
Strategic planner, House of Radon

German by origin, I have lived in Stockholm for five years and I truly love it. I spend my free time exploring concerts, museums, cafés, and restaurants and like to share what I find.

Our Legacy
P.054

Thommy Bindefeld
Creative director, Svenskt Tenn

I am responsible for the brand identity and securing the long life of this historical interior company built upon the philosophy of founder Estrid Ericson and architect Josef Frank.

Nick Ross
Founder, Nick Ross Design Studio

I run a design studio in the north of Stockholm. We work with furniture and lighting projects for commissions as well as research-based studio projects.

Stutterheim
P.052

Svenskt Tenn
P.056

Henrik Franklin
Animator, cartoonist & curator

I am a Konstfack graduate and one of the instigators of Book on the Fritz, a project that studies the morphology and development of publications through forums and exhibitions.

Papercut
P.059

Mathias Sterner
Photographer & director

I have a soft spot for mother nature's grand spectacles and spend a lot of time on Öland where I am originally from. My most recent fascination is plants. Growing stuff is pretty awesome!

Virpi Pahkinen
Choreographer & dancer

Born in Finland, I have performed on big stages and steppes in over 45 countries. I am a master of travelling with light luggage, and a believer of discipline with a lust for improvisation.

Rönnells
Antikvariat
P.058

Acne Studios
P.060

Björn Atldax
Cofounder, Vår & Cheap Monday

I grew up in Siberia and am one half of design firm, Vår. I was responsible for Cheap Monday's brand style and artwork. Now, I draw monsters, build sculptures of bones, freelance, and cook.

Brand-stationen P.062

Per Emanuelsson
Founder, Humans since 1982

I founded Humans since 1982 with Bastian Bischoff upon our graduation from Göteborgs Universitet (HDK). Our work has appeared at museums, galleries, and auctions worldwide.

Viktor Khan
Animator & illustrator

I am an animator, graphic designer, and illustrator residing in Stockholm. I animate dancing food items and hard-working cats, and sometimes, I do some serious work.

Södermalms Akvarieaffär P.061

Humana Second Hand P.064

Linnea Olsson
Cellist, singer & composer

I have released two solo albums under my own name and lived in Stockholm for two years, so the city is pretty new to me. I am slowly getting to know it.

Antikt Gammalt & Nytt P.066

Erik Bergqvist
Acne Advertising

I am a creative director, father of one, owner of a dog, and author of three books (all equally silly). I learnt my trade in London but moved back to Stockholm for the sake of love.

Ester Ideskog (Vanbot)
Artist & songwriter

I moved to Stockholm right after high school and have been in love with this city ever since. I perform as Vanbot and I do electronic pop music. I am a melody junkie!

Epok Antik & Kuriosa P.065

Hornstulls Marknad P.067

25 Stutterheim
Map E, P.107

Alexander Stutterheim launched his own brand of handmade raincoats as a homage to his late grandfather, whose old raincoat protected him on fishing trips out in Arholma. A wardrobe staple for many Stockholmers, this updated, contemporary version of the traditional rain-coat is versatile, hard-wearing, and designed to be a coat that is just as useful worn in the countryside as it is while strolling around the city. While in the area, enjoy a meal or drink at the cosy Söders Marley Café or Urban Deli.

🕐 1100–1800 (M–F), –1600 (Sa), 1200– (Su) 🏠 Åsögatan 132, 116 24
📞 +46 (0)8 408 103 98
URL stutterheim.com
f @stutterheimraincoats
◎ @stutterheim

"*Twice a year, Stutterheim has a big sale of samples and last season's colours. It is usually mayhem, but if you're lucky, you can score a real bargain.*"
– Lukas Rose, House of Radon

26 Our Legacy
Map I, P.109

For the more fashion-conscious traveller, a visit to Stockholm would not be complete without stepping inside Our Legacy. Known for its innovative yet understated menswear, the brand takes an inventive approach to fabric by infusing suits, workwear, and streetwear with distinct Scandinavian influences. Its artful minimalism has attracted a loyal following amongst Stockholm city dwellers and celebrities. To shop some more, pop into Nudie Jeans, a popular Swedish denim label, next door.

🕐 1100–1830 (M–F), –1700 (Sa), 1200–1600 (Su)
🏠 Jakobsbergsgatan 11, 111 44   📞 +46 (0)8 611 1010
🌐 www.ourlegacy.se   f @ourlegacy.se
📷 @ourlegacy   🖉 Opening hours vary by season.

"Visit the store on Jakobsbergsgatan to see the beautiful interior by Arrhov Frick."
– Nick Ross

27 Svenskt Tenn
Map D, P.106

Historical and contemporary interior design meet at Svenskt Tenn. Founded in 1924 by designer and drawing teacher Estrid Ericson, Svenskt Tenn is known for its lush and stunning textile designs by Josef Frank, an Austrian-Jewish architect who developed his own type of modernism as a nod to nature's wealth of colours and forms. Step into the store and take in the elegant furniture, wallpapers, and lighting – all produced by craftsmen in Sweden. It also holds exhibitions regularly. To take home a piece of classic Swedish design that truly suits your style, the staff offers expert advice.

🕙 1000–1800 (M–F), –1600 (Sa)
🏠 Strandvägen 5, 114 51
📞 +46 (0)8 670 1600
🔗 www.svenskttenn.se
📘 📷 @svenskttenn
🖉 Opening hours vary with holidays.

"Don't miss the tea room on the second floor."

– Thommy Bindefeld, Svenskt Tenn

28 Rönnells Antikvariat
Map A, P.105

One of Scandinavia's largest antiquarian book stores, Rönnells Antikvariat offers patrons the rare opportunity to explore beautiful things of the past. Opened in 1929, it houses over 100,000 books on every topic and genre imaginable; from art to music, and from fiction to 19th century travel guides. Spend an afternoon foraging through the sales rack and take home a unique piece of history with you. The chic Östermalm neighbourhood in which it is located also has a lot to offer: watch a movie at Zita Folkets arthouse cinema, take a leisurely stroll at the Humlegården park or grab a drink at Bird.

🕐 1000-1800 (M-F), 1200-1600 (Sa-Su)
🏠 Birger Jarlsgatan 32B, 114 29
📞 +46 (0)8 545 015 60
URL ronnells.se
f Rönnells Antikvariat

"They have a wide variety of different genres including a really great art book section. The pop-up bookstores from guest curators are also a very nice touch."
– Henrik Franklin

29 Papercut
Map I, P.109

Papercut is a self-professed 'magazine-junkie's paradise'. The shop stocks an outstanding selection of local and international publications for hobbyists, collectors, and the design-savvy. Avid readers will find everything from niche surf magazines to obscure fashion titles; from leading publications such as Monocle, Wallpaper*, and Vogue, to small independent titles like Deriva Paper and Four & Sons. It also offers a well-curated selection of books, music, and DVDs. After shopping, head over to Drop Coffee at Wollmar Yxkullsgatan 10, an award-winning roastery and café, for a pick-me-up.

🕐 1100-1830 (M-F), -1700 (Sa), 1200-1600 (Su)
🏠 Krukmakargatan 24-26, 118 51
📞 +46 (0)8 133 574   🔗 papercutshop.se
📘 @papercutstockholm 📷 @papercutshop

"The best selection in Stockholm when it comes to interesting publications, both foreign and domestic."

– Mathias Sterner

30 Acne Studios
Map D, P.106

The Swedes always seem to get 'effortless cool' right, and Acne Studios encapsulates the locals' distinct aesthetic and fashion-forward flair. Creative director Jonny Johansson's interests in contemporary culture, art, architecture, and photography are distilled into the Stockholm-based label's multidisciplinary approach, which results in eclectic yet exquisitely-executed ready-to-wear collections every season. It is also involved in special collaborations and projects such as exhibitions that bring forth its brand philosophy. Browse around any of their outlets for doses of style inspiration.

🕐 1000-2000 (M–F), –1800 (Sa), 1200-1700 (Su) 🏠 Hamngatan 10-14, 111 47
📞 +46 (0)8 203 455
URL www.acnestudios.com
f 📷 @acnestudios

"A jeans label that has grown into a global fashion brand, where Swedish cool slightly overtakes the 'lagom' or 'moderate is perfect' philosophy."
– Virpi Pahkinen

31 Södermalms Akvarieaffär
Map I, P.109

Södermalms Akvarieaffär is home to an impressive selection of aquariums, fish tanks, exotic fish, and fish-rearing related accessories. Stocked with all the equipment you could possibly require to keep your pet tropical fish happy, the owner is especially knowledgeable on the subject and has been known to keep customers enthralled in conversation for hours. An alternative and delightful way to spend an afternoon in Stockholm.

🕐 *1500–1900 (Tu–F), 1200–1600 (Sa–Su)*
🏠 *Krukmakargatan 3, 118 51* 📞 *+46 (0)8 441 0180*
🌐 *www.sodermalmsakvarieaffar.se*

basement is a geek's paradise – if your specialty is fish least. Go on a Tuesday before you hit the bars and have conversations that can last you the whole night."

– Björn Atldax, Vår & Cheap Monday

32 Brandstationen
Map I, P.109

Since 2005, Stockholm's favourite vintage clothing store Herr Judit has sought to champion high-quality products sourced from all over the world. Its interiors arm Brandstationen focuses on vintage furnishings and antiques, artfully curated for trendy and style-conscious connoisseurs. Tall windows flood the store with natural light, creating a calm and relaxing atmosphere for customers to browse around its growing collection of decorative objects and trinkets. It is a modern-day treasure trove of inspiring interior items infused with history.

🕐 1100–1800 (M–F), –1700 (Sa), 1200–1600 (Su) 🏠 Hornsgatan 64, 118 51
📞 +46 (0)8 658 3010
🌐 www.herrjudit.se/brandstationen
📷 @brandstationen_store

"There are two more vintage stores from the same owner up the street at Hornsgatan 65 and 75, which focus more on clothing."

– Per Emanuelsson, Humans since 1982

33 Humana Second Hand

Map I, P.109

Stockholm's leading thrift and vintage store Humana Second Hand offers a huge variety of clothing, shoes, and accessories at knockdown prices. With new stock added almost daily, the sprawling space caters to both women and men, attracting a mostly young crowd. Its parent company Humana Sweden is part of an international network of independent organisations working to create an equitable and sustainable society. Help yourself to their wide selection of secondhand goodies, while at the same time, making the world a better place.

🕐 1000–1800 (M–F), 1100–1700 (Sa), 1200–1600 (Su)
🏠 Timmermansgatan 23, 118 55
📞 +46 (0)8 640 4323
🔗 ⓞ humanasecondhand.se
📘 @HumanaSecondHand

"A really great vintage clothing store. Well-organised and has a great selection of clothes in great condition – and it's cheap!"

– Viktor Khan

34 Epok Antik & Kuriosa
Map A, P.104

Filled to the brim with beautiful vintage clothes and jewellery with a special section for wedding dresses and accessories, Epok Antik & Kuriosa is a true gem. The affable owner is highly knowledgeable about past styles, so don't be shy to ask questions about her pieces. After the nostalgic trip back in time, have a cup of coffee at the equally charming and retro Konditori Ritorno, which is just a few steps away, or stroll around the idyllic Vasaparken, one of Stockholm's most loved parks.

🕐 1100–1800 (M–F), –1500 (Sa)
🏠 Odengatan 83, 113 22
📞 +46 (0)8 341 340
📷 @epok_vintage

"Book ahead if you are looking for a wedding dress. You will get access to the room upstairs that is like an attic filled with vintage wedding bonanza."

– Linnea Olsson

35 Antikt Gammalt & Nytt
Map D, P.106

With a name that translates to 'Antiques Old and New', Antikt Gammalt & Nytt is the place to go for rare vintage accessories. The shop was opened by Tore and Mats Grundström when they discovered a warehouse full of long-forgotten 1940s jewellery. A popular spot for stylists and dedicated followers of fashion, be prepared to jostle for the best pieces. To complete your vintage experience, stop by Konditori Sturekatten, a quaint café located in a 18th century house nearby with ornate interiors resembling a fancy grandma's living room.

🕐 1100–1800 (M–F), 1200–1600 (Sa)
🏠 Mäster Samuelsgatan 11, 111 44
📞 +46 (0)8 678 3530

"Whatever you do, don't go there with a rucksack on your back. The place is small and I can promise you that you don't want to knock something over."

– Erik Bergqvist, Acne Advertising

36 Hornstulls Marknad

Map G, P.108

During the warmest months of the year, the Hornstulls waterfront in Södermalm bursts into life every weekend with a bustling 'loppis' (Swedish flea market) and gastronomic hotspot that locals flock to. At the Hornstulls Marknad, one can spend a fulfilling day hunting for vintage, contemporary, or handmade treasures after fuelling up at the various food stalls offering delicious traditional and trendy fare. As the latter's line-up changes weekly, it can get pretty crowded with chowhounds, but there will be plenty of places nearby for you to tuck into your takeaway meal by the riverside.

🕐 1100–1700 (Sa-Su) [Apr–Sept]
🏠 Hornstulls Strand 1-13, 117 39
URL www.hornstullsmarknad.se
f @hornstullsmarknad

"Bring cash, get there pretty early, and take your time – it's well worth it."

– Ester Ideskog (Vanbot)

Restaurants & Cafés

Cosy cafés, fancy meatballs, and fresh organic cuisine

Stockholm is often associated with its wealth of independent cafés and charming *fika* culture, which entails having coffee and something small on the side – be it a cinnamon bun, piece of cake, or *semla*. It can happen at any moment of the day, whether with family, friends or a special someone. As a whole, Swedish food culture is largely based on great access to local, fresh ingredients provided by a wealth of farmlands, forests, rivers, and lakes, as the locals are said to love picking herbs, berries, and mushrooms in the wild. Besides organic restaurants, the city is also dotted with modern pizza parlours, Thai kiosks, hamburger places, and popular hotdog stands. Start the day with a morning *fika* at Mellqvist Kaffebar (#45), a cosy spot close to the canal, then go for Hermans' vegetarian lunch buffet (*hermans.se*) - their terrace has a stunning view of Lake Mälaren and the city skyline. Peckish before dinner? You can't go wrong with a delicious specialty hotdog from street food vendor Günter's Korvar (#48). For your next *fika*, drop by award-winning Drop Coffee (*www. dropcoffee.com*) and admire their meticulous coffee preparation process. As the evening draws in, why not try traditional Swedish meatballs within a wood-panelled grand hall at Pelikan (#40), or sample some mouth-watering smoke-infused cuisine at Ekstedt (#38)? For a spot of romance or fine-dining with an affordable price tag, Oaxen Slip (#42) offers a memorable meal by the harbour.

Oaxen Slip, P.078

Fredrik Wetterholm
Cofounder, Another Agency

My partners and I run Another Agency for brands that want to digitise their businesses. I was born and raised in a Stockholm suburb and now live in the city with my wife and daughter.

Ekstedt
P.073

Catrin Vagnemark
Co-owner, BVD

Catrin Vagnemark is one of the first women to set up and lead a design bureau in Sweden and is still one of the leading creative directors in the business. BVD's philosophy is 'Simplify to Clarify'.

Sebastian Westin
Cofounder, Sandqvist

I am one of three founders of Sandqvist bags and items. I work as a PR and marketing manager. I love outdoor activities, fly fishing, motorcycles, and golf.

Nybrogatan
38
P.072

Ett Hem
P.074

Martin Nicolausson
Illustrator & graphic designer

Martin Nicolausson is perhaps the only Swedish illustrator and graphic designer with the name Martin Nicolausson.

Restaurang
Indian Inn
P.077

Johan Bring
Film director & photographer

I am a Swedish film director, photographer, screenwriter, gallery owner, and musician. I have lived in Stockholm since 1994.

Byggstudio
Graphic design group

Byggstudio is Hanna Nilsson and Sofia Østerhus who work mostly with interiors and public spaces. Nilsson has resided in Stockholm since 2008 and Østerhus in Oslo where she is originally from.

Pelikan
P.076

Oaxen Slip
P.078

Tony Cederteg
Libraryman & Tony Cederteg

I am the founder of photobook publisher Libraryman and design studio Tony Cederteg, as well as the founder and creative director of film/fashion magazine Dogme. I travel often for work and to retain sanity.

Falafelbaren
P.081

Carl Kleiner
Photographer

I am an image-maker – born, raised, and based in Stockholm. I am most noted for my still-life photography created for Ikea, H&M, WALLPAPER*, and AnOther Magazine.

Teenage Engineering
Product design studio

Teenage Engineering is a studio for future commercial products and communication. We create high-quality, well designed electronic products for all people who love sound and music.

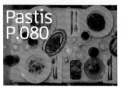

Pastis
P.080

Mellqvist
Kaffebar
P.082

Petter Johansson
Creative director & CEO, PJADAD

PJADAD works across disciplines independent of media. Recent works include IKEA's design collection "IKEA PS 2012" with a global multi-channel campaign.

**Östermalms
Saluhall**
P.084

Note Design Studio
Multidisciplinary design studio

Note works within within the fields of architecture, interior, product, and graphic design. Our philosophy is to stand out from the crowd: "To note something, to get noticed."

Marcus Lundin
Director

I am a commercial and music video director who was born in a small town in the northern parts of Sweden, and now live in Stockholm with my wife Caroline and son Kid.

Djuret
P.083

Günter's
Korvar
P.085

37 Nybrogatan 38
Map D, P.106

A popular neighbourhood restaurant that serves traditional Swedish dishes and old classics with a contemporary twist, Nybrogatan 38 will offer you slices of local life through ambience and taste. Tuck into a scrumptious breakfast, lunch, or late dinner here for a reasonable price. During the warmer months, opt for a table on the terrace and indulge in a tasty selection of crafted cocktails from the bar.

🕐 0730–2300 (M), –0000 (Tu–Th), –0100 (F), 1000– (Sa), –0000 (Su)
🏠 Nybrogatan 38, 114 40
☎ +46 (0)8 662 3322
URL nybrogatan38.com
🔲 Nybrogatan 38 🅾 @nybrogatan38
🖉 Check online for summer closure.

"Stockholm's best choice for breakfast, brunch, lunch or dinner. You may catch me and my friends spinning records in their bar on a Friday or Saturday."

– Fredrik Wetterholm, Another Agency

38 Ekstedt
Map D, P.106

Restaurant Ekstedt materialised from the bold idea of creating cuisine without any electricity, only flames. Everything is cooked over an open fire with wood sourced from Scandinavian apple trees, infusing each dish with a slightly smoky flavour. Order the blackened langoustine with squid and sea lettuce or hay-flamed beef with artichoke, and indulge in a lavish meal at one of Stockholm's hippest hangouts.

🕐 1800 till late (Tu–Th), 1700– (F), 1600– (Sa) 🏠 Humlegårdsgatan 17, 114 46 📞 +46 (0)8 611 1210
🔗 ekstedt.nu ⓕ @Ekstedt
ⓘ @ekstedtrestaurant
🔗 Reservations recommended. Book via website.

"*This is the opposite of molecular and futuristic gastronomy. Make sure to book in advance, preferably at least three weeks ahead.*"

– Sebastian Westin, Sandqvist

39 **Ett Hem**
Map A, P.105

Ett Hem is a luxurious boutique hotel with a low-key yet elegant ambience. Within the red-brick facade, its interiors present a sophisticated blend of contemporary and vintage design. To ensure that both staying and non-staying guests feel like they are in a private home, they are welcome to dine wherever they please, with choices including a lush greenhouse with views of the garden or the more formal library with striking features and fittings. The overall atmosphere is decidedly warm and intimate, making it an ideal destination for those looking to experience true hospitality in the city.

🕑 *Morning till late-evening daily*
🏠 *Sköldungagatan 2, 114 27* 📞 *+46 (0)8 200 590*
🔗 *www.etthem.se* 🔳 📷 *@EttHemStockholm*
🔖 *Reservations required for non-staying guests. Check hotel website for info.*

"An exclusive hotel with a fantastic restaurant."
– Catrin Vagnemark, BVD

40 Pelikan
Map E, P.107

Housed in a former beer hall in Södermalm, Pelikan serves up authentic Swedish home fare in a grand wood-panelled hall with high ceilings and old-world charm. Packed by early evening, the atmosphere is relaxed and lively, as diners take full advantage of their craft beer menu while waiting for their order. Try the *Grosshandlarvillan* dinner, a boiled knuckle of pork with mashed turnips and three kinds of mustard, or opt for a traditional dish of Swedish meatballs for a hearty meal. Wash everything down at its convivial bar area afterwards.

🕐 1700–0000 daily 🏠 Blekingegatan 40, 116 62
📞 +46 (0)8 556 090 90 🔗 www.pelikan.se
📘 Restaurant Pelikan 📷 @pelikan_sthlm

"*Don't be discouraged by some of the staff's lack of manners. It's part of the experience. Have SOS ('Sill och Snaps' or herring and snaps) and meatballs.*"
– Martin Nicolausson

41 Restaurang Indian Inn
Map G, P.108

Having undergone a recent revival of sorts, the Hornstull district in Södermalm has become a thriving cultural haven where many eateries and bars have taken up residence. For authentic Indian food, look no further than Indian Inn, which offers an eclectic menu using fresh ingredients and traditional spices. Bask in its interiors that are as delightful as the nosh served or dine outside during the warmer months, then work your meal off with a walk to Hornstulls Strand or the Tanto park.

🕐 1100–2300 (M–F), 1300– (Sa–Su)
🏠 Verkstadsgatan 11–13, 117 36
📞 +46 (0)8 668 9231/3
URL www.indianinn.se
f Indian Inn

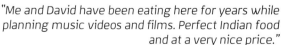

"Me and David have been eating here for years while planning music videos and films. Perfect Indian food and at a very nice price."
– Johan Bring

42 Oaxen Slip
Map B, P.105

Go on a little escape to Oaxen, a celebrated gastronomic destination on Djurgården that was established by chef Magnus Ek and his wife Agneta Green in 2013. Slip is in fact the casual half of the restaurant, serving up its own interpretation of Swedish bistro fare with unique ingredients sourced from the island as well as the Nordic region. Try the weekly specials that liven up the menu during the summer season. Next to Slip is Krog, a fine-dining gem in Stockholm with two Michelin stars. Oaxen Slip only has limited seats at the bar for walk-in guests, so be sure to book ahead.

🕐 1130–1600, 1700–2300 (M–F), 1500 till late (Sa–Su)
🏠 Beckholmsvägen 26, 115 21 📞 +46 (0)8 551 531 05
URL oaxen.com f ⓘ @OaxenSlip
🖉 Card payments only. Reservations recommended. Book via website.

"Take the boat from Slussen, then walk past the amusement park, lush greenery, and old houses to the harbour – getting there is half the joy."

– Hanna Nilsson & Sofia Østerhus, Byggstudio

43 Pastis
Map D, P.106

After a day of wandering around the historic Gamla Stan (#6), wind down with dinner at Pastis – a cosy and charming bistro serving tasty and reasonably-priced French classics in the heart of the Old Town. Its outdoor dining area and rustic interiors are reminiscent of those you would see in France itself, complemented by an array of dishes made with love. Go for the 'plat du jour' as you indulge in glasses of wine amid its intimate ambience. Should you have trouble reading the French menu, friendly waitstaff will be on-hand to help.

🕐 1600 till late (M–W), 1130 till late (Th–F), 1200 till late (Sa–Su)
🏠 Baggensgatan 12, 111 31
📞 +46 (0)8 202 018 URL pastis.se
🔗 Reservations recommended. Book via website.

"A hidden gem, even though it's so 'exposed' along the street in Stockholm's tourist mecca."

– Tony Cederteg

44 Falafelbaren

Map I, P.109

From haloumi fries to hummus, Middle-Eastern food fans will delight in the quality, portions, and affordability of the menu items at Falafelbaren. As its name suggests, the falafels are a must-try, with organic, gluten-free, and vegan-friendly options available for those with specific dietary requirements. Be sure to wash everything down with the refreshing home-made lemonade. Popular among locals, it has also been known to hold exhibitions within its cosy premises, so check online for updates or skip peak meal times to avoid the crowds.

🕐 1100–1900 (M–F), –1600 (Sa)
🏠 Hornsgatan 39B, 118 49
📞 +46 (0)7 2907 2637
URL www.falafelbaren.se
📘 @falafelbaren

"If the weather allows, ask for take-out and head to one of the parks nearby."

– Carl Kleiner

45 Mellqvist Kaffebar
Map A, P.104

A hip coffee bar with a tasty selection of freshly prepared food, drinks, and traditional Swedish snacks, the new(er) Mellqvist Kaffebar brims with the same unpretentious charm and chilled out vibes that it made it renowned at its previous location. Its bustling outdoor area is perfect for people-watching on sunny days, whilst the more intimate interior space is typically filled with students and freelancers working in peace or those indulging in cosy meals and conversations. A great pit stop before or after exploring the vibrant neighbourhood.

🕐 0600–2100 (M–Th), –1900 (F–Su)
🏠 Rörstrandsgatan 4, 113 41
📞 +46 (0)8 302 38
📘 Mellqvist Kaffebar
📷 @mellqvistkaffebar

"Coffee, food, and more."
–Teenage Engineering

46 Djuret
Map D, P.106

Inspired by seasonal produce from the land and sea, Djuret is all about maximising each fresh ingredient's gastronomic expression via specialist cooking techniques. The restaurant's three-course savoury menu based on a meat of choice is a perennial favourite, with vegetarian options available upon request. If you are dining in a large group, the Grand Deluxe menu consists of all the dishes in the house. Or, for something a little bit different, take part in the Walking Dinner to try its signature dishes as well as those of its sister restaurants and bars around the vicinity or 'gastroblock'.

🕑 1730–0000 (Tu–Sa) 🏠 Lilla Nygatan 5, 111 28
📞 +46 (0)8 5064 0084 🌐 www.djuret.se
📷 @rest_djuret 🖉 Walking Dinner:
1700/1730/1800 (Th–Sa) @2,500 SEK per person.
Book via website.

> "If you are lucky, you will meet
> the mythical and magical Jesper Kouthoofd
> (founder of Teenage Engineering)."
> – Petter Johansson, PJADAD

47 Östermalms Saluhall
Map D, P.106

The Östermalms Saluhall or market hall was built at the end of the 19th century. Housed in a red-brick structure with an iron frame and roof designed by prominent Swedish architect Kasper Salin, the 'temple of food' hosts a variety of delicatessen stalls, as well as those selling a wide assortment of cheese, sausages, game, and other delicacies. It is also famous for offering high-quality ingredients and cooked dishes from Sweden and beyond. Food lovers will delight in the seemingly endless choices of gastronomic delights here.

🕐 0930–1900 (M–F), –1700 (Sa)
🏠 Östermalmstorg, 114 39
URL www.ostermalmshallen.se
f @OstermalmsSaluhall
◎ @ostermalmshallen
🔗 Opening hours vary with holidays.

"You will find the best of Scandinavian food in this historical building."
– Note Design Studio

48 Günter's Korvar
Map A, P.104

A favourite with the locals, Günter's Korvar is said to offer the finest sausages in town. It serves them in a way that lies somewhere in between a French hot dog and a panino, where its 'bun' is a hollowed-out half-baguette that is grilled on a press and stuffed to the point of bursting with sausage meat and sauerkraut. Günter's extensive menu offers plenty of choices and combinations, so it is wise to have a back-up plan as favourites sell out quickly. Try the homemade chilli sauce if you're feeling brave, and enjoy your korvar in the sunshine.

🕐 1100-2000 (M–F), –1600 (Sa)
🏠 Karlbergsvägen 66, 113 35
📞 +46 (0)8 311 771
f Günter's korvar
🖉 Cash only

"This is where the locals queue up for the best sausages money can buy. The line might be long but Günter's homemade chimichurri will make up for the wait."

– Marcus Lundin

Nightlife

Excellent live music, parties under a bridge, and magical nightswimming

Over the years, the Swedish capital has really come to life as a party city of international standards. Nothing proves this better than the many open-air sessions that go on in and around the city on boats, in forests, and under bridges from dusk 'till dawn. Don't let the reserved and shy exterior of the Swedes fool you. When the alcohol is flowing, their true fun-loving nature comes out and you'd better be ready for the night of your life. The evening starts with a *förfest* (pre-party), as revellers gather in friends' living rooms with their Systembolaget-bought drinks. Alcohol is expensive in Sweden, especially at bars, so locals try to maximise the night by drinking at home with their less expensive stock from the government-regulated store before heading out to the pricier clubs. If you feel like a king, kick off the night with cocktails at fancy French bar Riche (#54) or Hawaiian-themed Tiki Room (#53). Then, ease yourself into the evening's entertainment at hip lounge bar Slakthuset (#51), and take in a gorgeous sunset at one of its many rooftop parties. Check out the gigs at Debaser Medis or Strand (#50), which are excellent venues for live music and touring acts. For a truly unforgettable experience, go to Trädgården (#49) which offers an awe-inspiring mix of dance floors, street food, and game areas nestled under a towering concrete bridge. Play ping pong, dance, meet new friends, and say 'yes' when they invite you to the after-party. To seal the night, take a dip in one of the city's many lakes. Långholmen (#60) is a good spot, but you can take the locals' lead. Float on your back and bask under the midnight sun – there's nothing quite like it.

Maja Gunn
Artist, designer & writer

My research studies fashion design methodology, while I design costumes for films and theatre. My tips are related to summer, as that is when I love Stockholm the most.

Debaser Strand
P.092

Cho Hyunjung
Founder, J0o0lry

Evident in the name, J0o0lry's mission is to explore within the scope of body-related artefacts using unreadable language. J0o0lry launched its first commercial project in 2014.

Lina Forsgren
Graphic designer & art director

I am a freelance graphic designer at Reform Act and I co-run Feministiska Kommunikations-byrån. I work across disciplines within different fields.

Trädgården
P.090

Slakthuset
P.093

Karl Grandin
Cofounder, Vår & Cheap Monday

After art directing for Swedish music magazine *Pop*, I set up Vår and Cheap Monday with Björn Atldax. Today, I freelance and do art projects, encompassing all things from drawings to alchemy.

Tiki Room
P.095

TWENTY-FIVE
25AH
ART HOUSE

25AH
Brand & design agency

25AH was founded by three friends from Forsbergs School of Design. Among our assignments, you will find strategic visual communication for advertising, branding, and exhibitions.

Clara Nordlander Wiberg
Cofounder, Francis Floor

I am a creative director and a Swedish champion in both artistic gymnastics and team gymnastics. My dad is my biggest inspiration. My life goal is to visit all countries in the world.

Mbargo
P.094

Riche
P.096

Brendan Austin
Photographer

Through fictional landscapes, I question how we perceive both the reality of the image and how we experience the world around us. I currently live in Stockholm with my wife and two sons.

**Häktet
P.098**

Fredrik Lund-Hansen
Cofounder, Rebels Studios

Parallel to my creative studio, Rebels Studios, I run the skateboard company Up South together with my friend Douglas Bielke. I used to live in New York but now I am back in Stockholm.

Agneta Green
Owner, Oaxen Krog & Slip

I live and work with my husband Magnus Ek on Djurgården where we run our restaurants. When I am off work, I go on long walks with our dog named Ringo Star, as he was born on the day we got our first Michelin star.

**Bleck
P.097**

**Babette
P.099**

Anna Giertz
Illustrator & musician

Originally from Gotland, I have been living in Stockholm for years where I work as an illustrator and musician.

**Night Camping
P.101**

Jonas Jacob Svensson
Photographer

My work falls within the fields of documentary and editorial photography, with a focus on portraits. I produce images for magazines and advertising. I am based in Stockholm but work wherever necessary.

Quiltland
Musician

I am a musician and a pattern cutter living in Stockholm.

**Omnipollos Hatt
P.100**

**Night-swimming at Långholmen
P.102**

49 Trädgården
Map E, P.107

Trädgården (Tree Garden) is an outdoor won-
derland which includes a bar, lounge, club, and
concert venue under a huge bridge in Skanstull. This one-of-a-kind space is where the
hipster youth of Stockholm gather throughout
the summer for ping pong, retro video games,
live performances, or partying 'till dawn. There
is also an art gallery on site. In the colder
months, Trädgården magically turns into Under
Bron (Under the Bridge), another cool crowd
favourite. Check online for programme info.

🕐 💲 *Opening hours & prices vary with events*
🏠 *Hammarby Slussväg 2, 118 60*
🔗 *www.tradgarden.com, www.husetunderbron.se*
📘 *@Tradgarden, Under Bron*

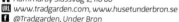

"This (partly) outside club is a must in the summer.
For daytime sessions, the party starts early – and it
always ends late."

– Maja Gunn

50 Debaser Strand
Map G, P.108

Tucked away in a basement along the waters of Hornstull Strand lies the intimate concert hall known as Debaser Strand. The venue has become a cult favorite amongst Stockholm's music lovers with its grungy atmosphere, small stage, and limited seating areas. Its bar has an industrial feel to it that suits the rest of the pared down interiors. Performances range from established names to up-and-coming live acts, so check online before heading over.

🕐 💲 *Showtimes & prices vary with programmes. Bar: 1800-0300 (F-Sa)*
🏠 *Hornstulls Strand 4, 117 39* 📞 *+46 (0)8 658 6350*
🔗 *debaser.se* 📘 *@DebaserSthlm*

"My favourites are the feminist club nights. In the summer, you can bring your own beer and sit outside on the small pier before you enter the club."

– Lina Forsgren

 ## 51 Slakthuset
Map C, P.105

Slakthuset is a renowned lounge bar and nightclub with a creative and artsy vibe, often frequented by the stylish and fashionable crowd. Located in the industrial district of Johanneshov close to the Ericsson Globe (#4), the 1,000-capacity venue offers an eclectic line-up of DJs playing house, deep bass, techno, underground, and hip-hop. Open all year round, its outdoor rooftop parties are especially popular, featuring special guest performances that will keep you moving from sunset till sunrise.

🕐 1700-0300 (F-Sa)
💲 Prices vary with events
🏠 Slakthusgatan 6, 121 62
🔗 slakthuset.nu 📘 @slakthuset
🔗 Check online for ticket info.

"Like most of the other clubs in Stockholm, things get more interesting after midnight. Check out their Facebook page for details on the night's event."

– Cho Hyunjung, J0o0lry

52 Mbargo
Map G, P.108

Located in the hip Hornstull area next to Austrian restaurant Moldau, this laid-back bar offers a great selection of reasonably-priced beers. Choices feature a range of Swedish and Danish microbrews, including familiar names like Omnipollo, Mikkeller, and Dugges Ale & Porterbryggeri. With an eclectic decor and a mixed clientele, Mbargo is a rare gem in a sea of fancy overpriced bars in the city. Grab a drink amongst the locals and feel welcome.

🕐 1800–0100 (M–Sa), –2200 (Su)
🏠 Bergsunds Strand 37, 117 38
f Mbargo

"Perfect for beers before or after dinner at restaurant Barbro, seeing a gig at Debaser Strand, or having drinks at Tjoget – all close by."

– Karl Grandin, Vår & Cheap Monday

53 Tiki Room
Map A, P.104

A trip to Tiki Room is akin to being teleported to the land of sun, sand, and sea in the middle of Stockholm. Its quirky interiors feature blowfishes on the ceiling, tribal masks on the wall, and a TV on the bar with 1970s surf films on repeat. Fun and fuss-free, the Hawaiian-themed bar offers killer cocktails and dancing till late. Music veers on the loud side, so if you prefer conversations over booming beats, head upstairs to the quieter Mellow Bar.

🕐 1800-0000 (M-Th), 1600-0100 (F), 1700- (Sa)
🏠 Birkagatan 10, 113 36   ☎ +46 (0)8 331 555
f @TikiRoomStockholm

"*Beware of the Volcano drink. It tastes like heaven but will give you hell! Sometimes that's good, and sometimes that's bad.*"

– Clara Nordlander Wiberg

 Riche
Map D, P.106

Founded in 1893, Riche strove to emulate
the legendary Café Riche on Boulevard des
Italiens in Paris, in decor as well as in character.
Starched linen tablecloths, elegant gold-
framed mirrors, and crystal chandeliers make
for a classic yet intimate venue in the heart of
the city. A popular spot to start the night before
hitting Stockholm's many clubs, weekends at
Riche can be loud and crowded, but generally,
it is upbeat, lively, and memorable. Be sure to
check out the artwork around the venue, created primarily by Swedish artists.

🕐 0730-0000 (M), –0100 (Tu), –0200
(W–F), 1100-0200 (Sa), 1200-0000 (Su)
🏠 Birger Jarlsgatan 4, 114 34
📞 +46 (0)8 545 035 60 🔗 riche.se
📘 @RicheStockholm

*"Stay all night or start your evening here before
heading off to the many clubs and bars around Riche."*
– 25AH

55 Bleck
Map E, P.107

Injecting some buzz into the quieter parts of Södermalm, restaurant Bleck offers a relaxed dining experience amid the lush and leafy setting of Lilla Blecktornsparken. A firm favourite amongst locals, the Johan Lytz–designed space serves a fine selection of gastro-inspired dishes complemented by an extensive beer and cocktail menu. Its friendly staff, idyllic surroundings, and affordable menu are the qualities that bring people back time and time again. Bleck operates a strict no-reservation policy, so just show up and be surprised.

🕐 1130 till late (Su–Th), –0100 (F–Sa)
🏠 Katarina Bangata 68, 116 42
📞 +46 (0)8 666 1234 **URL** restaurangbleck.se
ⓕ @restaurangbleck

"This place is best in the summer. Arrive early for a beer or wine on the courtyard overlooking the park."

– Brendan Austin

56 Häktet
Map I, P.109

Häktet Vänster is a hidden cocktail bar, serving up some of the city's best drinks. The word 'häktet' refers to 'jail' in Swedish, as the place was actually a prison back in 1781. Shrouded in an air of mystery, ring the bell before entering, and upon being buzzed in, climb up the stairs to enter the prohibition-era bar. Locals come here to kickstart their weekend with trendy cocktails, or after checking out Häktet's other dining concepts. The bar gets pretty crowded, so consider yourself lucky if you get in.

🕐 Vänster: 2100–0300 (W), 2000– (Th-Sa) [Häktet: 1500–0100 (M-W), –0300 (Th-Sa), 1700–2300 (Su)]
🏠 Hornsgatan 82, 118 21 📞 +46 (0)8 845 910
🔗 haktet.se 📘 @haktet

"On arrival, try to push the door on your left. If it's locked, it means the place is full. Otherwise, walk in and have a drink at this bar within a bar."

– Fredrik Lund-Hansen, Rebels Studios

57 Babette
Map A, P.105

A tiny restaurant and bar located in an area called 'Siberia', Babette offers a menu and wine list that changes regularly. Standard fare includes pizzas, snacks, starters, main courses, cheese, and dessert. Its excellent wine selection, combined with a warm and friendly atmosphere, make for a cosy and relaxing evening out. If you fancy eating somewhere else before getting drinks here, Sibiriens Soppkök along the same street is a family-run kitchen specialising in delicious soups.

🕐 1700 till late daily 🏠 Roslagsgatan 6, 113 55
📞 +46 (0)8 509 022 24 🔗 babette.se
📘 Babette, Roslagsgatan 6, Stockholm

'Magnus and I don't go out so much, but the staff often go here after we close. Each wine is purchased in small quantities and most run out in the same evening."

– Agneta Green, Oaxen Krog & Slip

58 **Omnipollos Hatt**
Map E, P.107

Rustic pilsners, new-school pizzas, and home-made pickles make up the gist of Omnipollos Hatt's magical gastronomic experience. Jointly owned by Swedish nomadic brewery Omnipollo and local pizzeria Pizzahatt, the space features unique touches by local artists whilst Cheap Monday and Ominipollo co-founder Karl Grandin leaves his mark on the beer bottle designs to match their delightful contents. Besides tucking into light and fluffy sourdough creations from the woodfire pizza oven, be sure to also try as many beers as you can, as many are exclusively served here.

🕐 1200-0100 daily 🏠 Hökens Gata 1A, 116 46
📞 +46 (0)7 2287 2224 🔗 www.omnipolloshatt.com
📘 @Omnipolloshatt

"Check the bathroom. There are plenty of delicate details to look at."
– Anna Giertz

59 Night Camping

For those with a taste for adventure, Sweden's *Allemansrätt* (Right of Public Access) is a unique institution that allows everyone the freedom to roam the stunning Swedish countryside on land and water – providing visitors do so respectfully. For short excursions, you can swim or sail almost anywhere, take scenic walks in the national parks and nature reserves, and climb a mountain or moor up on a tiny island in the archipelago. If you want more, visit the southwest suburb Bredäng for a night or two of camping, or go further out for a truly wild experience under the open skies.

URL www.naturvardsverket.se

"I promise you will find nothing alike in the city centre. So take advantage of the right of public access: tack your tent and go out into the woods."

– Jonas Jacob Svensson

60 Nightswimming at Långholmen

Map G, P.108

Steal a moment away from the endless parties in central Stockholm to experience the tranquillity of Långholmen. A popular hang-out for picnics, walks, and dips, the island is often described as a green oasis in the city. Float away on a night swim during the summer months, and enjoy the surrealistic charm that this spot has to offer. Combined with the stunning beauty of the midnight sun, nightswimming in Stockholm is a memory that will stay in your heart for a long time.

URL langholmen.com

"*Take off your clothes and let your make-up float away into the Mälaren. Don't forget to take in the view of the City Hall across the water.*"

– Quiltland

DISTRICT MAP : **VASASTAN, VASASTADEN**

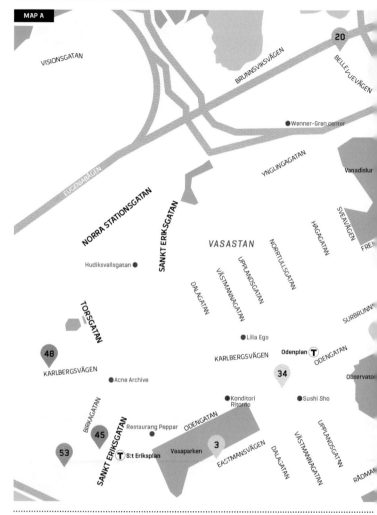

MAP A

- 3_Sven-Harrys Konstmuseum
- 5_Stockholms Stadsbibliotek
- 20_Carl Eldhs Ateljémuseum
- 34_Epok Antik & Kuriosa
- 45_ Mellqvist Kaffebar
- 48_Günter's Korvar
- 53_Tiki Room

MAP B

DJURGÅRDSVÄGEN

RUDDAMMSVÄGEN

HAZELIUSBACKEN

Skansen ●

21

FALKENBERGSGATAN

● ABBA The Museum

DJURGÅRDSVÄGEN

VALHALLAVÄGEN

NORDENSKIÖLDSGATAN

ROSLAGSGATAN

BIRGER JARLSGATAN

● Gröna Lund

BECKHOLMSVÄGEN

42

1000 ft.

ODENGATAN

39

MAP C

57

T Globen

4

PALMFELTSVÄGEN

VÄRDSGATAN

KARLAVÄGEN

STORA SKORSTENSGATAN

ARENAVÄGEN

REHNSGATAN

Adam & Albin ●
Matstudio AB

51

RÖKERIGATAN

KUNGSTENSGATAN

HALLVÄGEN

SLAKTHUSGATAN

DÖBELNSGATAN

Un Poco ●

BOSKAPSVÄGEN

EVÄGEN

T Rådmansgatan

HALLVÄGEN

BIRGER JARLSGATAN

NERGATAN

KAMMAKARGATAN

28

LINT

Biografen Zita Folkets
Bio Stockholm ●

1000 ft.

TRÄDSKOLEVÄGEN

1000 ft.

● 4_Ericsson Globe

● 39_Ett Hem

● 57_Babette

● 21_Liljevalchs

● 42_Oaxen Slip

● 28_Rönnells Antikvariat

● 51_Slakthuset

DISTRICT MAP : **NORRMALM, ÖSTERMALM, GAMLA STAN, SKEPPSHOLMEN**

MAP D

- 6_Gamla Stan
- 16_Moderna Museet
- 22_Hallwylska Museet
- 27_Svenskt Tenn
- 30_Acne Studios
- 35_Antikt Gammalt & Nytt
- 37_Nybrogatan 38
- 38_Ekstedt
- 43_Pastis
- 46_Djuret
- 47_Östermalms Saluhall
- 54_Riche

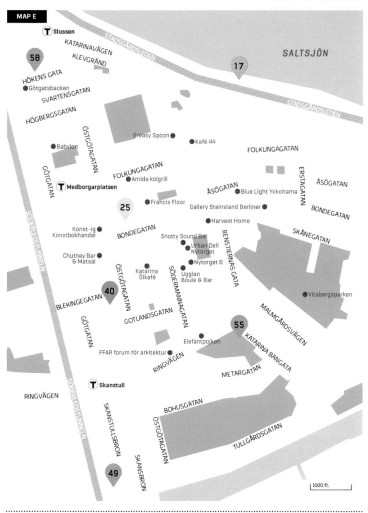

MAP E

T Slussen

KATARINAVÄGEN

STADSGÅRDSLEDEN

KLEVGRÄND

SALTSJÖN

58

17

HÖKENS GATA

● Götgatsbacken

STADSGÅRDSLEDEN

SVARTENSGATAN

HÖGBERGSGATAN

ÖSTGÖTAGATAN

Greasy Spoon ●

● Kafé 44

FOLKUNGAGATAN

● Babylon

GÖTGATAN

FOLKUNGAGATAN

ERSTAGATAN

ÅSÖGATAN

T Medborgarplatsen

● Amida kolgrill

ÅSÖGATAN

● Blue Light Yokohama

25

● Francis Floor

Gallery Steinsland Berliner ●

BONDEGATAN

Konst-ig
Konstbokhandel

BONDEGATAN

● Harvest Home

SKÅNEGATAN

Snotty Sound Bar

RENSTIERNAS GATA

Chutney Bar
& Matsal ●

ÖSTGÖTAGATAN

● Urban Deli
Nytorget

40

● Katarina
Ölkafé

SÖDERMANNAGATAN

● Nytorget 6

● Ugglan
Boule & Bar

● Vitabergsparken

MALMGÅRDSVÄGEN

BLEKINGEGATAN

GOTLANDSGATAN

GÖTGATAN

55

● Elefantpojken

KATARINA BANGATA

FFAR forum för arkitektur ●

RINGVÄGEN

METARGATAN

T Skanstull

RINGVÄGEN

SKANSTULLSBRON

BOHUSGATAN

ÖSTGÖTAGATAN

TULLGÅRDSGATAN

SKANSBRON

49

1000 ft.

● 17_Fotografiska

● 49_Trädgården

◐ 25_Stutterheim

● 55_Bleck

● 40_Pelikan

● 58_Omnipollos Hatt

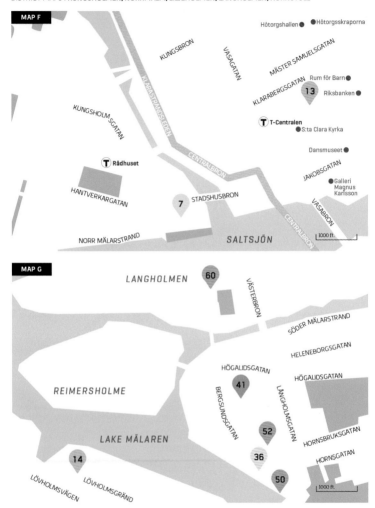

- 7_Stadshuset
- 13_Kulturhuset Stadsteatern
- 14_Färgfabriken
- 36_Hornstulls Marknad
- 41_Restaurang Indian Inn
- 50_Debaser Strand
- 52_Mbargo
- 60_The Cliffs of Långholmen

MAP H

MAP I

- 2_Filmhuset
- 11_Skinnarviksberget
- 18_Magasin III
- 24_Seriegalleriet
- 26_Our Legacy
- 29_Papercut
- 31_Södermalms Akvarieaffär
- 32_Brandstationen
- 33_Humana Second Hand
- 44_Falafelbaren
- 56_Häktet

DISTRICT MAPS : **SUNDBYBERG, VÄRMDÖ, KRISTINEBERG, JOHANNESHOV, HÄGERSTEN, ENSKEDEDALEN**

- 8_Markuskyrkan
- 9_Skogskyrkogården
- 10_Tranebergsbron
- 15_Artipelag
- 19_Marabouparken
- 23_Kulturföreningen Tellus

Accommodation

Hip hostels, fully-equipped apartments & swanky hotels

No journey is perfect without a good night's sleep to recharge. Whether you're backpacking or on a business trip, our picks combine top quality and convenience, whatever your budget.

 < 800 SEK 801–1600  1601+

Ett Hem

A former private residence built in 1910, Ett Hem provides cosy and tranquil accommodation steeped in Scandinavian aesthetics. Discerning guests will enjoy the comfortable interiors, spacious suites, and courtyard garden. Besides a fully-equipped gym, traditional Swedish sauna, and hot stone slab, it also offers wonderful dining experiences (#39).

🏠 *Sköldungagatan 2, 114 27*
📞 *+ 46 (0)8 200 590* 🌐 *www.etthem.se*

Scandic No. 53

Previously known as HTL Kungsgatan, Scandic No. 53 is a three-star boutique hotel with modern rooms and a no-fuss approach that ensure a comfortable stay at a reasonable price. Its convenient location places the Royal Castle, Gamla Stan, and the waterfront all nearby.

🏠 *Kungsgatan 53, 111 22* 📞 *+46 (0)8 517 365 00*
URL *www.scandichotels.se/no53*
💲

Miss Clara

Housed in an Art Nouveau building, Miss Clara is a boutique hotel that was originally built as the Ateneum girls' school in 1910. It features inherently stylish rooms without compromising on comfort – highlighted by dark herringbone parquet floors and industrial materiality. All public areas are wheelchair accessible, with rooms customised for special needs.

🏠 Sveavägen 48, 111 34 📞 +46 (0)8 440 6700
🔗 missclarahotel.com

Hotel J

🏠 *Ellensviksvägen 1, 131 28*
📞 *+46 (0)8 601 3000*
🔗 *hotelj.com*

Hotel Skeppsholmen

🏠 *Gröna Gången 1, Box 1616, 111 86*
📞 *+46 (0)8 407 2300*
🔗 *www.hotelskeppsholmen.se*

Notes

Index

Petter Johansson @PJADAD, p083
pjadad.com

Tony Cederteg @Libraryman, p080
www.libraryman.se,
www.tonycederteg.com
Portrait by Kristian Bengtsson

Industrial

Clara von Zweigbergk, p021
www.claravonzweigbergk.com
Portrait by Kaisu Juoppi

David Ericsson, p024
davidericsson.se

FORM US WITH LOVE, p020
www.formuswithlove.se

Nick Ross, p054
nckrss.com

Note Design Studio, p084
notedesignstudio.se

Teenage Engineering, p082
teenage.engineering

Music

Ester Ideskog @Vanbot, p067
www.vanbotmusic.com
Portrait by Sara Arnald

Linnea Olsson, p065
FB: @linneaolssonmusic/

Quiltland, p102
soundcloud.com/quiltland

Performing Art

Virpi Pahkinen, p060
www.pahkinen.com
Portrait by Mattias Lindbäck

Photography

Brendan Austin, p097
www.brendanaustin.com

Carl Kleiner, p081
www.carlkleiner.com

Jonas Jacob Svensson, p101
www.behance.net/onasja-cobsvensson

Mathias Sterner, p059
www.mathiassterner.com

Photo & other credits

Djuret, p083
(All) instagram.com/foodi-eguidesthlm

Ekstedt, p073
(p070 & 073 Lobster tail & steam)
PA Jorgensen; (p073 Table set &
wine shelves) MathiasNordgren

Ericsson Globe, p018
(p012 & 018 Bottom) Ola Ericson/
imagebank.sweden.se

Ett Hem, p074-075
(All) Ett Hem

Färgfabriken, p035
(p035 Interior) Färgfabriken
(p032 & 035 Exterior & meeting
room) Åke E.son Lindman

Filmhuset, p016
(p012 & 016 Exterior) Mark Standley

Hallwylska Museet, p044-045
(p045 Grand salon & smoking
room) Erik Lernestäl, Hallwylska
Museet; (p045 Exterior & dining
table) Arild Libra, Hallwylska
Museet

Kulturhuset Stadsteatern,
p034
(p034 Sofa) Petra Hellberg

Magasin III, p040
(p030, 032 & 040 Man & ball)
Christian Saltas; (p040 Exterior)
Jesper Nordström

Night Camping, p101
(Camp & kayak) Henrik Trygg/
imagebank.sweden.se

Nybrogatan 38, p072
(Interior & facade) Nybrogatan

Oaxen Slip, p078-079
(All) Erik Olsson, licensed to
Creative Commons erkännande/
mynewsdesk.com

Östermalms Saluhall, p084
(Exterior) Raphael Cameron

Our Legacy, p054
(p050 & 054 Top) Our Legacy

Pelikan, p076
(Wall painting & food) Pelikan

Riche, p096
(Exterior, bar & mussels) Niklas
Alexandersson, licensed to
Creative Commons erkännande,
inga bearbetningar/mynews-
desk.com

Skogskyrkogården, p025
(All) Licensed to Creative Com-
mons erkännande/mynewsdesk.
com; (Corridor, candle & sunset)
Susanne Hallman; (Stairs) Mikael
Almehag

Stadshuset, p021-023
(p021 Golden Hall) Ola Ericson/
imagebank.sweden.se; (The
Nobel Prize) Jeppe Wikstrom/
mediabank.visitstockholm.com;
(River) Anna Andersson/image-
bank.sweden.se; (p022-023) Björn
Olin Folio/imagebank.sweden.se

Stockholms Skärgård, p029
(p029 House) Ola Ericson/image-
bank.sweden.se; (Boat) Conny
Fridh/imagebank.sweden.se;
(Kayak & dog) Henrik Trygg/
imagebank.sweden.se

Stockholms Stadsbibliotek,
p019
(Middle) Simon Paulin/image-
bank.sweden.se

Stockholms Tunnelbana,
p014-015
(p010, p014 Escalators & p015
Rainbow) Kevin Kee Pil Cho/
imagebank.sweden.se

Stutterheim, p052
(p050 & p052 All) Stutterheim

Sven-Harrys Konstmuseum,
p017
(Exterior) Licensed to Creative
Commons erkännande/mynews-
desk.com; (Entrance) Per Myre-
hed; (Side view) Ola Fogelström

Tranebergsbron, p026-027
(p027 Snow White, The Little
Mermaid & Hello Kitty) Herr
Nilsson

In Accommodation: All courtesy
of respective hotels.

CITIX60

CITIx60: Stockholm

First published and distributed by
viction workshop ltd

viction:ary™

7C Seabright Plaza, 9-23 Shell Street,
North Point, Hong Kong

Url: www.victionary.com
Email: we@victionary.com
🅵 www.facebook.com/victionworkshop
🐦 www.twitter.com/victionary_
📷 www.instagram.com/victionworkshop

Edited and produced by viction:ary

Concept & art direction: Victor Cheung
Research & editorial: Queenie Ho, Caroline Kong
Project coordination: Jovan Lip, Katherine Wong
Design & map illustration: Frank Lo, MW Wong, Leanne Lee, Scarlet Ng

Contributing editor: Angel Trinidad
Contributing writer: Lisa Hassell
Cover map illustration: Gustav Dejert
Count to 10 illustrations: Guillaume Kashima aka Funny Fun
Photography: Gerard Puigmal

Content is compiled based on facts available as of July 2019. Travellers are
advised to check for updates from respective locations before your visit.

First edition
ISBN 978-988-79726-9-3
Printed and bound in China

Acknowledgements

A special thank you to all creatives, photographers, editors, producers, com-
panies, and organisations for your crucial contributions to our inspiration and
knowledge necessary for the creation of this book. And, to the many whose
names are not credited but have participated in the completion of the book,
we thank you for your input and continuous support.

CITIX60
City Guides

CITIx60 is a handpicked list of hotspots that illustrates the spirit of the world's most exhilarating design hubs. From what you see to where you stay, this city guide series leads you to experience the best — the places that only passionate insiders know and go.

Each volume is a unique collaboration with local creatives from selected cities. Known for their accomplishments in fields as varied as advertising, architecture, graphics, fashion, industrial design, food, music, and publishing, they are at the cutting edge of what's on and when. Whether it's a one-day stopover or a longer trip, **CITIx60** is your inspirational guide.

Stay tuned for new editions.

City guides available now:

Amsterdam
Barcelona
Berlin
Copenhagen
Hong Kong
Istanbul
Lisbon
London
Los Angeles
Melbourne
Milan
New York
Paris

Portland
San Francisco
Singapore
Stockholm
Taipei
Tokyo
Vancouver
Vienna